The Summer Party

by Jessica Lee Anderson
Illustrations by Colleen Madden

Sara and Mom planned to go to Sweden! Sara had an uncle and an aunt who lived there.

"Let me show you how we will get to Sweden," Mom said. "Look at this map. We will fly over this big sea."

Sara and her mom got on a plane.
The trip was long.

At last, they landed in Sweden.
Aunt Anna and Uncle Lars met them.
They hugged Sara.

"You will have fun here," said Uncle Lars.

"You have come just in time," said Aunt Anna.

"In Sweden, we have a festival.
It is on the first day of summer.
This big party is in two days!"

Sara liked the home where her aunt and uncle lived.

She was happy about the festival, too.
Mom helped cook for the festival.
Sara helped, too.
They made so much food!

Festival day was here!
Mom helped Sara get ready.
They put on nice clothes and picked flowers.
Mom made a flower crown for Sara.

Then they all went to the park.

"There is the Maypole," said Mom.
It was a tall pole.

A song started to play.
Sara and her mom danced.

Her aunt and uncle danced, too.

Then they all did a Maypole dance.
"This is fun!" said Sara.

Soon it was time to eat.
The food was yummy.

At last, it was time to head home.

"The festival was fun!" said Sara.
"I will dance in my dreams."